W9-BID-373

Horse Club

by Patricia J. Murphy

LONDON, NEW YORK, MUNICH,
MELBOURNE, AND DELHI

DK LONDON
Series Editor Deborah Lock
US Editor Margaret Parrish
Production Editor Francesca Wardell
Project Art Editor Hoa Luc

Reading Consultant
Linda Gambrell, Ph.D.

DK DELHI
Editor Nandini Gupta
Assistant Art Editor Yamini Panwar
DTP Designer Anita Yadav
Picture Researcher Sumedha Chopra
Deputy Managing Editor Soma B. Chowdhury
Design Consultant Shefali Upadhyay

First American Edition, 2014
Published in the United States by
DK Publishing, 345 Hudson Street, New York, New York 10014

14 15 16 17 18   10 9 8 7 6 5 4 3 2 1
001—195875—January/2014

Copyright © 2014 Dorling Kindersley Limited
All rights reserved
Without limiting the rights under copyright reserved above, no part of this publication may be
reproduced, stored in or introduced into a retrieval system, or transmitted, in any form, or by any means
(electronic, mechanical, photocopying, recording, or otherwise), without the prior written permission of
both the copyright owner and the above publisher of this book.

Published in Great Britain by Dorling Kindersley Limited.
A catalog record for this book is available from the Library of Congress.

ISBN: 978-1-4654-1723-7 (pb)
ISBN: 978-1-4654-1811-1 (plc)

DK books are available at special discounts when purchased in bulk for sales promotions, premiums,
fund-raising, or educational use. For details, contact: DK Publishing Special Markets, 345 Hudson Street,
New York, New York 10014 or SpecialSales@dk.com.

Printed and bound in China by South China Printing Company.

The publisher would like to thank the following for their kind permission to reproduce their photographs:
(Key: a-above; b-below/bottom; c-center; f-far; l-left; r-right; t-top)
1 Pearson Asset Library: Gareth Boden. **5 Dreamstime.com:** Tchernyaeva8 (b). **11 Pearson Asset Library:**
Gareth Boden (cra). **21 Pearson Asset Library:** Naki Kouyioumtzis (b). **22 Pearson Asset Library:**
Naki Kouyioumtzis (b). **24 Corbis:** David Chapman / Design Pics (tl). **32-33 Dreamstime.com:** Isselee (c).
35 Dreamstime.com: Isselee (br). **45 Dreamstime.com:** Cherkas (br). **46 Dreamstime.com:** Yobro10 (tl).
Pearson Asset Library: Naki Kouyioumtzis (tr). **50 Dorling Kindersley:** W&H Gidden Ltd (tc). **64 Corbis:** ABK
/ BSIP (b). **65 Corbis:** ABK / BSIP (br). **Getty Images:** Boston Globe (cl). **66 Corbis:** Kit Houghton (bl).
67 The Long Rider's Guild (www.thelongridersguild.com / www.aimetschiffely.org): (tr). **80 Corbis:** Stapleton
Collection (cl); The Gallery Collection (cr). **81 Corbis:** Bettmann (bl). **90 Getty Images:** Photodisc / Thomas
Northcut (cr). **92 Alamy Images:** Moviestore collection Ltd (cr). **94 Getty Images:** Archive Photos / Moviepix
(l). **95 Getty Images:** Mondadori (bl); Archive Photos / Moviepix (tr, cr). **98 Corbis:** Jasper Cole / Blend Images
(bl). **106 Pearson Asset Library:** Coleman Yuen (cb). **109 Corbis:** Stefanie Grewel / cultura. **111 Corbis:** Dan
Rowley / Colorsport (tl); Michele Eve Sandberg (cr). **112 Alamy Images:** South West Images Scotland (c). **113
Getty Images:** Danita Delimont / Gallo Images (tl). **114 Corbis:** Kit Houghton (l). **115 Alamy Images:** Marn
Gorin (cl). **Getty Images:** Alexis Duclos / Gamma-Rapho (bl). **119 Corbis:** Sandra Seckinger
Jacket images: Front:
All others (c) Dorling Kindersley

All other images © Dorling Kindersley
For further information see: www.dkimages.com

Discover more at
www.dk.com

Contents

Chapter 1

Horse Dreams

While waiting for a batch of cupcakes to cool, Emma finished the horse drawing she had started earlier in the afternoon. She chose the dark-brown colored pencil to color in the body of the horse and used black for its mane, eyes, and tail.

"Now, if only you were a real horse, I'd ride you until my saddle and reins crumbled like a cookie," Emma sighed, as she added the finishing touches to her drawing and closed her notebook.

This was not just any notebook. It was the place where Emma collected her thoughts, feelings, ideas, recipes, and drawings. She recorded things about horse breeds, how she could help wild horses, and pasted her favorite horse pictures from *Horse Illustrated* magazine. Tucked inside was her collection of assorted flyers, brochures, and postcards of horse stables, academies, and shows in the area. It was also the place where she wrote about her horse dreams.

From the time Emma and her older sister, Amanda, rode their first horse-stick ponies, and then rode real ponies as part of summer camp, they had dreamed of riding together in a horse show one day and winning all kinds of ribbons.

"Of course," Amanda would say, "I'd lead us into the arena, do some amazing tricks—and you could be my sidekick."

Emma would roll her eyes and say, "I believe that I would be the one to do the tricks, you would be my sidekick—and I'd win a ribbon for my fabulous horseback riding skills."

While that dream had not come true just yet, Emma knew she would always be Amanda's sidekick. Always. But that was fine by her. For now, she could finally join the school's Horse Club, just like Amanda, and maybe move closer to fulfilling their dream. It was a club that her favorite teacher, Mrs. Bauer, had started a few years ago and Amanda was this year's club president.

HORSE CLUB
Meeting today
4:30 p.m.
in Room 7

Unfortunately, over the past year, the club had experienced its share of ups and downs, but not from riding horses. With the lack of time and funds, the Horse Club members hadn't done much more than research their favorite horse breeds, host an unsuccessful horse fair, debate which wild horse sanctuary to raise funds for, and talk about attending a horse camp some day. Emma would change that! They needed someone to take the reins and the next steps.

"Maybe I could spice things up a bit," pondered Emma, thinking about the Horse Club as she put the cayenne pepper away that she had used to add a "kick" to the red velvet cupcake batter.

To accomplish such a feat, Emma would switch her cooking hat for a thinking cap and come up with some fresh-baked ideas. But, right now, she had to finish her shift at her family's bakery, Sweet Dreams, and get home in time for dinner and homework.

Once home, Emma showered off the day's baking ingredients and curled up in her favorite thinking spot. She worked on finishing her homework: ten math problems, a writing assignment on the best way to frost a cupcake, and two chapters of *National Velvet*. (It was the third time she was reading this book!)

After Emma had added her favorite cream-cheese frosting recipe to her piece of writing, she fished out her special notebook from her backpack and started to brainstorm some ideas for her first Horse Club meeting next week. As she flipped through her notebook for a clean page, a loose postcard flew out and landed on her horse slippers. It was an ad about the Paddock Promises Horse Academy and Stables.

Paddock Promises

HORSE ACADEMY AND STABLES

777 South Paddock, Promises Lane, Country Club Hills

Where Your Horse-Sized Dreams Become Reality!

Located on more than 50 acres of prime paddock, trails, and farmland, we are your premier location for horseback riding lessons, training, shows, boarding, and more!

With our indoor and outdoor arenas, award-winning instructors, and world-class horses with the hearts of champions, we have two questions for you.

1. Why learn, train, show, or board anywhere else?
2. What are you waiting for?

Here are just some of the top-notch services we provide:

- **Private lessons** (for beginner, intermediate, and advanced riders)
- **Group lessons** (for beginner, intermediate, and advanced riders)
- **School groups**
- **Birthday parties, vacation parties, office parties, etc.**
- **Boarding**
- **Training**
- **Shows**

"Where your horse-sized dreams become reality!" Emma repeated as she typed in the website address on the computer and skimmed the website.

She read about the Paddock Promises "heralded" horse history, private and group lessons, and summer camps. Then she spotted a banner that ran across the website that said:

**PLACES STILL AVAILABLE
at the
VACATION HORSEBACK
RIDING CAMP
starting DECEMBER 26–31.**

Emma's head grew dizzy and she nearly fell out of her chair.

"That's it!" Emma steadied herself and printed out the information about the camp. She would make copies at school and present the idea at the Horse Club meeting when the right moment presented itself.

Emma knew the vacations were insanely busy at Sweet Dreams, but from the day after Christmas through to New Year's Day, the bakery was closed. It was perfect timing.

"Timing in life and baking is everything," Emma's mother would always say when things happened the moment you hoped they would.

Emma flipped back to the page of her recent horse drawing. She added Amanda and herself on the back of the horse.

"Maybe it's our time," Emma whispered, "for our horse-sized dream to become a reality!"

?

What ideas would you suggest if you attended a Horse Club meeting?

Know Your Horse

Here are the names of the different parts, or points, of a horse. They are useful to know when learning to handle, groom, tack up, and ride.

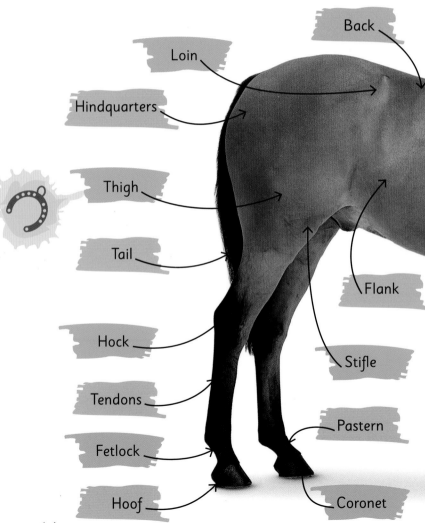

Back

Loin

Hindquarters

Thigh

Tail

Hock

Tendons

Fetlock

Hoof

Flank

Stifle

Pastern

Coronet

Mane

Ears

Neck

Forelock

Withers

Muzzle

Nostril

Shoulder

Chest

Forearm

Ribs

Elbow

Knee

15

Cupcake Recipe

This is the basic recipe for all Sweet Dreams cupcakes. For the red velvet cupcakes, add a dash of cayenne pepper, unsweetened cocoa, and red food coloring.

CAKES

- 10½ tbsp unsalted butter, softened
- ¾ cup granulated sugar
- 1¼ cups self-rising flour
- 3 medium eggs, whisked
- ½ tsp pure vanilla extract

ICING AND DECORATION

- 2½ cups confectioner's sugar, sifted
- 2–3 tbsp hot water
- food coloring
- cake decorations

1 Line two 12-cup muffin pans with baking cups. Preheat the oven to 350°F (180°C).

2 Place the butter, sugar, self-rising flour, eggs, and vanilla extract in a bowl and beat with a spoon until pale and creamy.

3 Divide the mixture between the baking cups. Bake for 15 minutes, until golden and just firm. Cool in the pan for 5 minutes, and then transfer the cupcakes to a cooling rack.

4 Once cool, trim any pointed tops to make a flat surface.

5 Put the confectioner's sugar in a large bowl and slowly stir in enough water to make a smooth, thick icing. Add a few drops of food coloring.

6 Spoon the icing onto the tops of the cupcakes. Add decorations. Alternatively, mix butter, cream cheese, and sugar to make a creamy frosting.

Chapter 2

One Heart

"You can't wear the same horse sweatshirt and turtleneck as me to the meeting," said Amanda, as her face turned the shade of Sweet Dreams' best-selling cherry pie. "Take them off immediately!"

"Come on, Amanda!" pleaded Emma, as she pulled her hair into a braid like her sister's. "We'll look official—you the president, and me, your loyal assistant."

"And take that braid out this instant," demanded Amanda. She started to undo it herself when their mother walked in to the room.

"Oh, Emma," her mother whispered, "Remember what we talked about?"

Emma sighed, "Having my own individual style. Trying to be myself."

"What if the two of you compromised a bit?" suggested their mother, trying to lighten the mood with her horse pun.

Emma and Amanda laughed at their mother's joke, and at themselves.

"I'll just wear the turtleneck," Emma said, as she took off the sweatshirt, "with my horseshoe earrings."

"You can keep the braid," said Amanda. "Just wear a different ribbon, all right?"

"All agreed, say: aye! All opposed, say: neigh!" Emma's mother neighed.

"Neigh!" Emma joked. "I mean, aye."

Amanda tugged Emma's braid, "Thanks, Emma-doodle!"

?

Why do you think
Emma wants to dress in
the same way as her sister?

"Welcome to the first Horse Club gathering of the new school year," began Mrs. Bauer, adjusting her horse scarf, as she called the meeting to order. "We're pleased to add new members to our herd."

In addition to Emma and Amanda, there was Bess, Amanda's best friend, Kiffin, Bess's sort-of-boyfriend, and two girls that Emma had seen around school. The one named Olive was in Emma's math class.

"This year, we're hoping to do some actual riding," announced Amanda. Her tone sounded hopeful. "Does anyone have any suggestions?"

Mrs. Bauer looked around the group. Emma took a deep breath and circulated copies of the postcard and information from the Internet.

"There's a place called Paddock Promises Horse Academy and Stables. It's only 45 miles away," explained Emma, twirling her braid, "and they have a vacation camp over the winter break."

Amanda's eyes brightened, "Wherever did you find this, Emma-doodle? I mean Emma. Why didn't you say…"

Mrs. Bauer interrupted, "Since there's no time like N-O-W, I'll make calls and get permission slips."

"I'll make a list of everything we'll need," said Amanda, grabbing a pen.

"Seems like this year's Horse Club is off on the right hoof," said Mrs. Bauer. She nodded toward Emma.

Boots

Jeans

Sweaters

After two months of extra evening and weekend shifts at Sweet Dreams, Emma and Amanda had enough money to attend Paddock Promises camp.

As they finished packing, Emma and Amanda checked the list one last time.

If Emma and Amanda hadn't had an endless supply of the last item, balancing school and the extra shifts at Sweet Dreams would have been crazy. But they were crazy… about horses.

Boots

Jeans

Sweaters

Underwear

Jacket

$100 camp fee

Love of horses!

The bus ride took an hour in snowy traffic. Emma quizzed Amanda on the "points" of a horse.

"You never know," said Emma, studying a horse chart she had taped to her special notebook, "when they might come in handy, especially this week."

"I hope it's just like the postcard says," said Amanda, looking out the window.

Emma crossed her fingers. They both knew how recipes didn't always look or turn out like the pictures in cookbooks.

"Maybe," Emma pointed to the horse's many types of leg markings, "it'll knock our socks off!"

?

What do you imagine
Paddock Promises
will be like?

When they arrived at Paddock Promises, the red barn was frosted with a layer of white.

"It looks like a red velvet cupcake," Emma whispered to Amanda. "It's a sign that we're supposed to be here!"

A round woman with a toothy grin welcomed them as they barreled off the bus.

"My name's Pearl Paddock and welcome to Paddock Promises Horse Academy and Stables!"

Pearl led them through the tidy barn's office, past the unending trophy case, and on a quick tour.

"You can look at our trophies more closely later," Pearl stopped for a moment. "We're proud of our accomplishments, but prouder of our promise." Pearl pointed to a sign on the wall:

Where your horse-sized dreams become reality!

"We hope to turn campers into life-long riders," Pearl continued, "and spread some horse-love along the way. After all, horses are amazing creatures. They deserve our love."

She sniffed. "Now, grab your keys, unpack your bags, and be back here in two shakes of a horsetail!"

Amanda handed Emma her bag. "I have to meet Mrs. Bauer to iron out the fees, permission slips, and checkout times. Meet me back here, okay?"

Emma unpacked in her room like a racehorse. She used half of the drawers and closet and then dashed out the door.

As Emma galloped back to the barn, Olive, a mass of curls and freckles, yelled to her.

"Hold your horses!" Olive panted. "What's your hurry?"

"It's been a while since I've ridden," Emma said, increasing her gait.

"Race you!" Olive half-joked.

The two sprinted all the way to the barn door.

"Now that everyone's here," Pearl said after counting heads, "please take a copy of the camp agenda and get ready for the rides of your lives!"

A gaunt, ruddy-faced woman in dusty jodhpurs stood next to Pearl; she was holding a clipboard. Pearl introduced her, "I call her my Lucky Penny. You'll call her Miss Penny. She's been teaching and training here since she retired from winning every competition she entered…"

"Oh, don't stop! I mean stop," Penny interrupted. "Thanks for that introduction, Pearl. Annie, my assistant instructor, and everyone at PPHAS are committed to making your stay: Pleasing, Promising, Happening, Award-winning, and Safe. But it'll be up to you to get the most out of it."

"Today, we'll fit helmets, meet-and-groom your horses, enjoy a welcome banquet, and watch a demonstration of our top riders. Please follow Annie and watch your step."

Annie, a slip of a woman wearing a *Got Horses?* sweatshirt, black tights, and muddy boots, led the way to the tack room. Emma felt like Goldilocks trying on helmets. The first was too big. The second was too small. The third was just right according to Annie, even though it pinched Emma's forehead. She didn't mind. She was so close to meeting *her* horse.

"Please greet your horses from the front, act confident yet caring. Let them see how grateful you are to be with them!" Penny said as she demonstrated. She explained how each horse and rider was matched according to the surveys they had filled out.

"Emma, meet Cinnamon." Penny pointed to the horse in stall number 33. "She's sweet and gentle. She'll do what you want and ask you to push yourself. She'll need someone who'll be up to new challenges—and not give up."

With the weight of the helmet, Emma tried to nod, but couldn't.

As she entered stall number 33, Emma saw standing before her the bay horse she had drawn in her notebook. It had the same dark brown body, and black tail and mane. Her dark brown eyes held Emma's and didn't look away.

"Hi, Girl!" Emma said, as she allowed Cinnamon to sniff her hand. "You don't know how long I've waited for and imagined this moment."

Cinnamon nuzzled under Emma's neck. Emma kissed Cinnamon's forehead.

"She can tell you're a true horse lover," Penny said, handing Cinnamon's grooming kit to Emma.

"Every brush has a different job," Penny explained to everyone. "The curry comb loosens dirt. The hard dandy brush removes it. The soft brush buffs and shines, and the base brush is for the face and legs. And since we learn by doing, let's *groooom*!"

Penny grabbed a dandy brush, "Tomorrow, like Pearl said, we'll begin those rides of your lives."

"Yes, indeed," said Pearl, joining the grooming party. "The type of rides where horse and rider share one heart!"

Horse Sense

Horses are sensitive to tones of voices, noises, and movements. Here are some top tips on how to meet, speak, touch, and move around your horse, helping to build a good relationship.

INTERPRETING MOOD

Ears pricked forward means your horse is attentive, willing, and bold.

Flattened back ears means anger.

Ears back suggests your horse is discontented or aware of something going on behind it.

Step 1
Let your horse see you.
Approach calmly, speaking
with a quiet voice.

Step 2
In a calm voice, tell
your horse what you
are going to do and
where you are.

Step 3
Run your hand over your
horse's back and quarters
as you move to walk
behind. Warn your horse.

Step 4
Use your touch and
tone of voice to soothe,
encourage, or guide
your horse. Don't rush.

31

Horse Grooming

Are you baffled by all the brushes in your groom kit? No worries. We have supplied a guide to them below!

Sponge
After brushing, gently wipe around the eyes, nostrils, and muzzle. Use another sponge for cleaning under the tail.

Damp water brush
Use to flatten the mane against the neck and the short hairs at the top of the tail.

Hoof pick
Scrape out any mud and stones, working from the heel toward the toe.

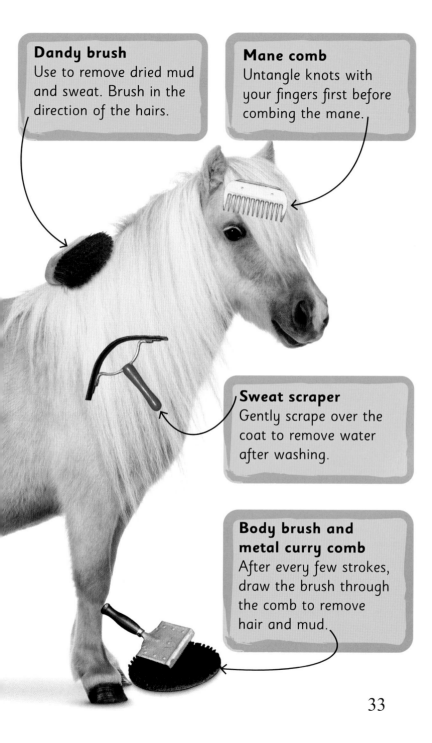

Dandy brush
Use to remove dried mud and sweat. Brush in the direction of the hairs.

Mane comb
Untangle knots with your fingers first before combing the mane.

Sweat scraper
Gently scrape over the coat to remove water after washing.

Body brush and metal curry comb
After every few strokes, draw the brush through the comb to remove hair and mud.

33

Horse Breeds

Each breed of horse has its own unique character and appearance. These characteristics could be strength, speed, toughness, endurance, size, or color. Every breed is part of a "type," describing its main use.

Akhal-Teke
Desert type with speed, endurance, and a light, long body.

Camargue
Rugged, intelligent, and calm with a strong, compact body.

Cleveland Bay
Docile, hard, and strong with muscular legs, withers, and shoulders.

Connemara
Stamina for long distances, intelligent and surefooted for jumping.

Haflinger
Energetic and proud with a light, short body and rhythmic movement.

Danish Warmblood
Friendly, tough, and bold with muscular head, neck, and legs on a tall body.

Kathiawari
Desert warhorse-type with affectionate, high spirits and inward curving ears.

Percheron
Proud and alert, willing worker, and a tall, sturdy body with muscled feet.

Quarter Horse
Versatile and calm with a sense of fun and a tall, powerful body.

Shetland
Hardy, gentle, and headstrong with a small, solid body.

Chapter 3
Close Call

Emma crawled out of bed for the third time to check the alarm clock. "At last it's morning and time to get up!"

"Go back to sleep!" Amanda mumbled. "It's still dark. We don't ride until 8:00 a.m."

"I'll be quiet," whispered Emma, fumbling for her horse slippers.

In record time, Emma showered and pulled her hair back into a ponytail. She opened the bathroom door a crack and used the light to find her horse bag, and then headed out.

Dawn was Emma's favorite time of the day. She especially loved the way today's sunrise gently kissed the farm, the barn, and… the horses. Some horses, dressed in their plaid PPHAS blankets, were already running and playing in the outdoor arena.

"Oh, my!" Emma's pace quickened, "Some horses are up as early as I am!"

Emma found a seat on the cold, metal bleachers. She pulled on her woolly hat and scarf to watch the horses. Emma waved at Penny already hard at work.

"Well, aren't you up early?" remarked Penny, waving a gloved hand at Emma. "Another sign of a true horse lover!"

Emma smiled under her scarf.

"Good morning, Girl!" Emma greeted Cinnamon as the horse passed.

When Cinnamon passed by a second time, she seemed to recognize Emma. Emma felt her heart skip a beat.

"Just like Velvet Brown felt in *National Velvet*," Emma gasped, "when she first saw the horse of her dreams."

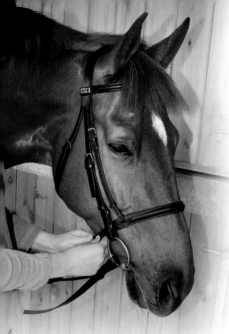

After a morning of instructions about putting on a bridle and saddle, Emma was able to bridle and saddle Cinnamon with only a little help and a whole lot of care. She remembered to warm the bit in her hands before placing it in Cinnamon's mouth and to double-check the tightness of the girth. Cinnamon was ready to ride.

"Half of you will be with Pearl for the 'Healthy Riders, Healthy Horses' course, and half will be tested on your riding skills. Then we'll switch," Penny directed. Annie counted half of the group and Pearl led them away.

"We'll be observing the rest of you: how you sit in the saddle, control your horse, and how comfortable and confident you appear," Penny explained.

"These elements will help us put you into the right group for the 'Horse Show-and-Tell' show."

"That's our end of camp demonstrations for your families," Annie added, "but more about that later."

First in line, Emma climbed up the mounting block to mount Cinnamon. Her stomach flipped, then flopped. She put her left foot into the stirrups, swung her right leg around, and sat tall on the saddle. Annie adjusted Emma's stirrups and instructed her to say, "Walk on!" and to press her calves gently into Cinnamon's sides.

At first, Emma and the others walked one at a time around the arena. Penny and Annie checked their grips on their reins and asked them to stop, turn, and reverse direction. Emma had forgotten how it looked high atop a horse and how her legs felt wrapped around 1,300 pounds (600 kilograms) of animal. She took a few deep breaths in and out.

The Right Riding Position

Sit deep and central in the saddle. A strong, well-balanced sitting position is essential for communicating with your horse during a ride.

1. Head
Keep your head up and look straight ahead. There should be no tension in your neck.

2. Arms
Keep arms relaxed; hold reins apart. Your elbows to the bit should form a straight line.

3. Shoulders to heels
Hold shoulders naturally and level. There should be an imaginary line to your heels.

4. Knee to toe
Slope your lower leg slightly so that your knee and toe are in line.

Keep your arms relaxed and hold the reins slightly apart.

Keep the balls of your feet on the stirrups with toes forward and heels down.

Rear view
Sit centrally in the saddle with feet level so a straight line is formed from your head to the end of the tail.

"Make sure your eyes are looking between the ears of your horse and be aware of what's going on around you at all times," coached Penny, standing in the center of the arena. Annie was on horseback.

As Emma completed a few laps around the arena, she felt more confident and even comfortable.

But, in a flash, the horse in front of Emma started to whinny, kick up his back leg, and head right toward Cinnamon!

Upset, Cinnamon started to whinny in response and throw back her head as if she wanted to do the same... or worse.

"Shorten the reins, Emma," Annie hollered, "and say, 'Whoa!'"

Emma did everything Annie instructed, but Cinnamon kept throwing her head back, kicking, and backing up.

"I'd like to get off now!" cried Emma. Her eyes looked alarmed and her heart raced. Her hands and feet began to sweat and she felt like she was going to faint.

"You'll be all right," Annie rode alongside Emma. "Cinnamon was just flustered by the other horse. Their routines have been different because of the vacation but they appear to be calming down now."

"I'dddd still like to dismount," Emma stammered.

"What if I stayed by your side?" Annie prodded. "If Cinnamon acts up again, we'll dismount and walk our horses. Do you trust me?"

"Yes." Emma's heartbeat started to return to normal.

"Then let's show Cinnamon," Annie encouraged, "who's really in charge!"

Emma couldn't wait to dismount and stand on sandy ground. After all the drama, she hightailed it back to the dorm. She felt as though she might cry.

"Maybe I should just pack up and head home," Emma thought to herself. As she started to dial her mother, someone knocked on the door. Emma looked through the peephole. It was Annie.

"This is from Cinnamon," said Annie, holding out a horse-shaped cookie and a mug of hot cocoa. "She's sorry that she upset you."

"Thanks," replied Emma, letting Annie inside her room.

"Tomorrow I'll be right beside you if you need me," said Annie, handing Emma the cookie first. "I promise that Cinnamon and the others will be on their best behavior and you can dismount anytime you want."

Emma bit the head off the horse cookie and laughed. Annie laughed, too.

"Yum!" Emma washed the cookie down with some cocoa. She tasted a dash of cinnamon.

"Is Cinnamon all right?" asked Emma, hoping she was.

"She's fine and when you are," Annie headed toward the door, "we're in the mess hall going over horse points and playing some 'Horse Body Bingo'!"

"Amanda and I were quizzing each other on the points on the way here!" Emma exclaimed, jumping to her feet and quickly finishing the tail end of her cookie. Annie looked surprised.

"Withers, forearm, flank, free space, leg, fetlock, muzzle, mane," Pearl repeated. "That's a good bingo."

Amanda leaped out of her chair to claim her prize. She picked the Paddock Promises pin with two horses running side by side. They reminded her of Emma and herself.

"Wait until I tell Emma!" Amanda looked around. "Where is she?"

When Emma walked in two bingo games later, Amanda flagged her over.

"Can you believe it? I just won!" Amanda smirked. "It seems that knowing horse points does come in handy."

"Good for you!" Emma tried to sound excited, but her tank was empty.

"Are you okay? You look as though…" Amanda stumbled for the right words.

"As though I was thrown from a horse? I wasn't… but it was a close call!" Emma felt the frightening feelings rush back as she replayed the darkest details.

"I'm so sorry, Emma!" Amanda fastened the PPHAS' pin on Emma's fleece and hugged her. Emma didn't want her to let go.

?
How do you think
Emma is feeling?

Dressed For Success

This riding gear and tack is a rider's dream for yourself and your horse.
Ride out in style!

1.Bridle
Quality leather with raised noseband and buckle fastenings

2.Hard hat
Padded helmet with traditional velvet, peak-shield design

3.Safety vest
Custom-fitted vest for maximum protection and comfort

4.Gloves
Close-fitting soft suede gloves for a firm and sensitive grip

5.Jodhpurs
Lightweight with inside-leg reinforcements for comfort and good grip

6.Boots
Classic long waterproof riding boots with nonslip soles

7.Saddle
Fully adjustable, quick-clean, all-purpose for rider and horse comfort

8.Saddle cloth
Nonslip pad that evenly cushions and protects your horse's back

Saddle Up!

Saddle cloth
or numnah

Saddle

1 Approach your horse's near-side shoulder with the saddle over your left arm. The pommel should be toward your elbow and girth and straps laid over the top.

2 Lift the saddle up above the withers and lower gently onto your horse's back. Make sure the hair is lying flat underneath.

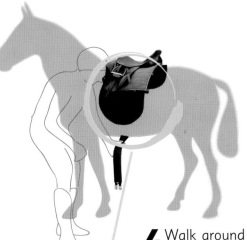

3 Slide the numnah and saddle back into position just behind the withers. Always slide in the direction of the hair.

4 Walk around the front of your horse to the other off side. Check that the numnah is lying flat. Let down the girth and check that it is straight.

5 Back on the near side, reach under the belly for the girth. Lift up the saddle flap and do up the buckle. Tighten the girth gradually and evenly on both the near-side and off-side buckles.

6 Smooth the hair under the girth and make sure that the skin is not pinched or caught anywhere. You should be able to slide three fingers underneath the girth.

Chapter 4

The Right Ingredients

Emma made a mental list while she mounted Cinnamon: (1) mount gently; (2) sit upright; (3) stay balanced; (4) hold the reins properly; and (5) don't get thrown off!

"I never thought," Emma said to Olive, trying not to think around yesterday, "that horseback riding was such a thinking sport—until, well… you know."

"I know," replied Olive. "There's a lot to remember and to do. It's like doing long division in math class!"

Emma and Olive shared a laugh.

"You're absolutely right," agreed Annie, adjusting Emma's stirrups.

"A lot of it becomes easier with practice and experience. But you must *always* keep your wits about you."

Emma hoped she would, too. As she steadied her reins, Emma followed her beginning group in turning right, then left, slowing down and speeding up.

"You're all following the directions nicely," encouraged Penny.

Emma calmed her nerves by talking to Cinnamon. "I have to do a lot of that when I'm baking things at my family bakery," said Emma, rubbing Cinnamon's side. "Did you know that cinnamon's a very versatile spice?"

"I like the way many of you are using sweet, gentle voices with your horses," said Penny, winking at Emma as she passed by. "That's how you bond, earn their trust, and take new steps."

Emma popped up like a Sweet Dreams popover. Maybe she did have the right ingredients for horseback riding after all, she thought.

"Next up, we're going to try posting and then trotting," Penny announced, as Annie rode into the center of the arena to demonstrate. "You post by using your legs to lift up slightly off your saddle and then gently lowering down."

Emma was the third rider to try. She lifted herself up and then down.

"Up-down!" she whispered to herself.

"Posting's the first step to trotting," Penny explained, "which is a two-gaited run."

Run? Emma wasn't sure if she wanted to start running with Cinnamon just yet. She pictured the horse in *National Velvet* running amok all over town.

"The second step is to tell the horse to trot," Penny instructed.

"Trot!" commanded Annie, trotting around the arena.

"Our volunteers will help anyone who wants assistance," said Penny.

Both Emma and Olive raised their hands high. Emma was happy

she wasn't alone in requesting help.
A tall boy with baggy jeans and warm
eyes helped Emma.

"Okay," Seth instructed, "tell
Cinnamon to trot."

"Trot!" Emma tried to do her part.
Cinnamon did hers.

"Up-down, up-down!" Seth repeated
as he ran alongside the pair.

"I feel likeeee I'm onnnn a hoppity-
horse onnnn the mmmerry-go-rrround!"
exclaimed Emma, hopping up and down.

"Try lifting as Cinnamon's inside
foreleg hits the ground," Seth pointed
out, "and *gently* sitting when her outside
foreleg does the same."

"Easy for you to say!" Emma thought
to herself. The constant ups and downs
hurt Emma's bottom. She tried to put
the ache out of her mind and follow
Seth's suggestions.

"Look at you, Emma," Seth called out,
"you're trotting!"

After trotting, or at least trying to, for the remainder of the class, Emma and the others watched Annie preview the canter.

"The canter is a three-beat gait," Annie demonstrated. "It's a smoother, faster ride than the trot and something you'll learn as you develop as a rider."

"… a life-long rider," added Penny, pointing at the Pegasus wall clock, "but, now, we must switch classes. It's time for the advanced beginners to ride."

"Please lead your horses back to their stalls, cool them down, and feed and water them," Annie announced, "—except Emma. Please give Cinnamon to Seth and come and join me."

Emma dismounted. Her legs felt wobbly and her hands shook as she gave the reins to Seth.

"Is something wrong?"

"Just the opposite," Annie grasped her clipboard. "We like the way you recovered from yesterday, your gallant effort today, and the relationship you're building with Cinnamon."

"Wow! I mean thanks!" exclaimed Emma. Her eyes sparkled.

"So I'd like you to join Cinnamon and me to help a group of children with special needs who benefit from working with horses," Annie shared.

"I'm in," said Emma, raising her hand.

"Hurray!" Annie cheered. "Meet us at the instructors' table after lunch."

Emma floated out of the arena and ran to tell Amanda.

"Up top!" Amanda high-fived Emma over the stall door as she finished mucking out Pepper's stall. "I wish I were *you* right now!"

"Can you say that again?" Emma giggled and grabbed Amanda's pitchfork. Nothing could ruin her double batch of bliss, not even a little (or a lot of) horse poop.

"Welcome, Still Water Center riders! Our horses, handpicked volunteers, and staff are thrilled to have you here," said Annie to the group of children.

After brief introductions, Emma glued herself to Cinnamon's left shoulder. She would help Seth lead Cinnamon with a rider, Molly, who had special needs.

"Molly, we need you to put your left foot in the stirrup and swing your right leg around and put your right foot in the other stirrup," said Seth, helping her.

Annie and Molly's special teacher, Mrs. Grace, took turns teaching the lesson.

"Hold on to the reins, honey," Mrs. Grace reminded, "and sit nice and tall."

With a nod from Annie, Emma and Seth

began leading Cinnamon around the arena.

"Now," Mrs. Grace instructed, "try hitting the colored balls as you and Cinnamon pass them."

Molly swatted the balls after a few reminders.

"Good girl!" Annie coached. "Now, let's play a bowling game. Can you hit one of the wall targets with the stuffed animals?"

Molly hit three targets. Molly, Emma, and Seth cheered softly.

Just then, one of the other students made a high-pitched sound. Hearing it, Cinnamon stirred.

"It's all right," Emma said, as she rubbed Cinnamon's shoulder. "Just someone having an extra good time."

Annie smiled. "Looks like I chose the right camper for this job."

Emma smiled back.

"Who wants to play 'Red light, Green light'?" Annie asked.

"When the stoplight on the wall flashes red, we say 'Whoa' and gently pull on Cinnamon's reins to stop," Annie explained.

Annie handed Emma the control for the stoplight. "You're in charge now." Emma flipped the stoplight to red. Molly sat still.

"Red light," Emma reminded.

"Whoa!" said Molly, gently pulling her reins with help.

"Hurray!" Emma said softly, as she switched the light to green.

"Green light," Seth chimed in.

"Tell Cinnamon to 'Walk on,'" Annie encouraged, "and give her a gentle squeeze with your legs."

"Walk on," Molly said, as Annie and Mrs. Grace helped her squeeze her calves into Cinnamon's sides.

"Way to go, Molly!" Emma and Molly tapped high five. "Let's tell Cinnamon that she did a good job, too!"

Emma showed Molly how to pat Cinnamon, and then changed the light to red.

"Whoa!" Molly said, as she lightly pulled Cinnamon's reins and flashed a smile that lit up the entire arena. Emma felt goose bumps on her arms and legs as she helped Molly dismount.

"Thanks to everyone who helped today," Annie hollered.

"Thank *you*!" Emma gushed. "I won't forget this!"

"I hope not," Annie shook her head. "Maybe you could join us another time."

"Green light!" Emma switched the stoplight from red to green.

Perfect Paces

How can you and your horse keep in perfect pace? Check out the four basic paces below... and practice, practice, practice!

Walk

At least two feet are on the ground at the same time. Each stride is equal length.

Walk

The sequence is four even foot falls: near hind, near fore, off hind, and off fore.

Canter

This is a three-time beat and there is a moment when all four feet are in the air.

Canter

For right-hand canter, the off legs lead, then near hind, off hind, and near fore.

Trot
The legs move in diagonal pairs with a moment of suspension.

Trot
The sequence is a two-time pace: off fore and near hind, near fore and off hind.

Gallop
This pace has the most extended stride length and has four foot falls.

Gallop
For right-hand gallop, the off fore leads, then near hind, off hind, near fore, and off fore.

Paddock Promises

HORSE ACADEMY AND STABLES

777 South Paddock, Promises Lane, Country Club Hills

Hippotherapy courses

Horses can help to treat children and adults with special needs. The rhythmic movement of a horse helps to strengthen and develop a rider's physical and mental abilities. Paddock Promises offers an ideal environment and well-equipped facilities with calm, friendly horses, highly trained staff, and caring volunteers.

Our Hippotherapy classes can help with:

 increasing body strength and control,

 balancing weight and building endurance,

 stimulating the senses of touch and sight,

 promoting emotional well-being.

Why a horse?

A horse's walk is rhythmic and repetitive, and the speed can be varied. This movement is similar to a person's movement of the pelvis while walking. This pattern of movement stimulates the rider's senses.

Within our natural setting, riders respond enthusiastically to this enjoyable experience.

Our trained professionals can vary the speed of the horse's walk and the activities to match the level of sensory stimulus appropriate to individual rider's specific needs.

The Story of Mancha and Gato

In 1925, Aimé Tschiffely, a Swiss teacher living in Argentina, had the crazy idea to be the first person to ride from Buenos Aires to Washington, D.C. He needed two tough horses to succeed on this very ambitious 10,000-mile (16,000-km) journey. He chose Mancha and Gato, who belonged to a Native Argentinian chief and who knew how to survive in the wild. In April, they set off. They quickly learned to trust each other and to work as a team as they faced the daily challenges of the trip.

Criollo horses
Wild Criollo horses, such as Mancha and Gato, form strong bonds.

On their treacherous journey through rivers, jungles, and over mountains, they were alert to many dangers, such as quicksand, snakes, and crocodiles. Gato and Mancha saved Tschiffely's life on many occasions.

Two and a half years after setting out, they arrived in Washington and were welcomed as heroes.

The route that Aimé Tschiffely took from Argentina to the United States of America.

Aimé Tschiffely with Mancha and Gato

Washington, D.C.

Ecuador
A landslide had swept away the path, leaving a sheer drop. Mancha was the first to leap over.

Andes Mountains
Mancha and Gato stayed calm as Tschiffely led them across a rickety old bridge above a deep gorge. One slip would have been fatal.

Buenos Aires, Argentina

67

Chapter 5

Forever Changed

Emma slept later than usual. She had hoped to see Cinnamon before breakfast as usual, but her hopes were dashed when she saw Annie leading her back to the stables.

"Horse feathers!" Emma turned around and headed to breakfast.

"Do you want to help cool down and feed Cinnamon?" Penny yelled from the stable, as she carried in bales of hay. "You missed your chance yesterday. Seth can show you how."

Emma ran all the way to the stables. She spied Seth mucking out a stall.

"I'll be right back to help you," said

Seth, wheeling a wheelbarrow full of steaming horse poop past her.

In the next row, Emma heard Cinnamon banging her stall door.

"She must have heard my voice," Emma thought to herself.

"I'm coming!" Emma said, as she spied Cinnamon hanging over her stall door, waiting like an old friend. Emma would miss these early morning meetings.

Seth reappeared.

"To cool her down," directed Seth, "we attach her to these cross ties, untack her, use this scraper to remove sweat, and then sponge her eyes and nose."

"Roger that!" Emma followed Seth's instructions. "You sure know your way around a stable," remarked Emma, filling up Cinnamon's water bucket. "You should work here…"

"I do," Seth admitted. "My last name's Paddock." He winked as he left the stall.

Emma's mouth dropped. She had had no idea. Cinnamon whinnied.

69

Stable Care

A clean, dry stable and healthy food will keep your horse content and energized. Muck out the stable every day after giving your horse breakfast. Keep the yard neat, too.

Wheelbarrow

Boots

Shaving rake

Rake

Pitchfork

Broom

Four-
pronged
fork

Shovel

Skip

Hose

Feeding
A stabled horse
needs to be fed
three times a day
with a mix of food
for energy, good
digestion, and a
shiny coat.

Root vegetables
and fruits

Coarse mix of corn,
oats, and sugar beets

Chaff:
chopped-up hay

Pellets made up of
different grains

71

Emma finished with the scraper and started with the sponge, "Have I told you how much I love you today, Cinnamon? Well, I love you, I do!" Cinnamon's lips appeared to curl into a smile.

"She sure has taken to you," Penny said, filling Cinnamon's haynet. "I haven't seen her respond to other riders quite like she does to you."

"Honest?" Emma cleaned Cinnamon's eyes and nose. "Cinnamon has stolen my heart. It'll be hard to say goodbye."

"Like Miss Pearl says: *'When horse and rider share one heart!'* You two are forever changed," Penny persisted. "You must come back for lessons or to help with our special riders. We'll have more this summer.

Consider this your invitation!"

Emma slathered saddle soap on Cinnamon's saddle, "Every summer, I work in the bakery…"

"You don't have to decide now," said Penny, polishing Cinnamon's bridle. "We'll call you when we start making our summer plans."

"I couldn't afford regular lessons," Emma confessed. "Amanda and I pulled double-shifts just to get *here*."

"Maybe," Penny proposed, "we can work something out for both of you. The special riders would love to see you again—and so would Cinnamon."

Cinnamon's ears perked up.

"You don't think," Emma pondered, crinkling her nose, "that she…"

"I don't think; I know," Penny whispered. "Now, go and get some breakfast. Cinnamon's other half needs to be well fed, too!"

Emma hugged Cinnamon and hurried to breakfast.

"Amandaaaa!" Emma gasped, unable to catch her breath. "We might be able to take lessons here, and…"

"Tell me later," Amanda interrupted, "Bess and Kiffin are telling me about a trail-riding party tomorrow night."

"Sounds like fun," Emma said excitedly. "Can I come?"

"It's for the older, more advanced riders," Amanda explained. "Besides, don't you think we've had enough sister time for a while?"

Bess and Kiffin laughed. Amanda did, too. Emma couldn't believe Amanda would say such a thing in front of Bess and Kiffin, and laugh! Tears stung Emma's eyes. She turned away, and made a beeline for the breakfast buffet.

"Nice drawing," Emma said, as she plopped down by Olive.

"Where have you been?" Olive asked, sharpening a pencil. "It's almost time for our morning session."

"Woooo-hooooo!" Pearl grabbed the

mess-hall microphone. "We sure have a horse-sized riding agenda today, with our morning skill practices for the 'Horse Show-and-Tell' and a sneak-preview of the 'Fun and Games' challenges to be held tomorrow. Some I did as a girl!"

"Miss Pearl's right," Penny added. "So let's not waste another second. Be sure to pick your partner by today. Also, any pairs interested in performing a challenge for the 'Horse Show-and-Tell,' go and see Seth."

Emma's thoughts immediately turned to Amanda. "But she'd probably pick Bess or…"

"Want to partner with me?" Olive asked, hoping Emma would say yes.

"You're sweet to ask, but Amanda and I have been dreaming of being in a horse show together since… forever," Emma tried to explain. "Although now, I'm not so sure she still has that dream…"

"You mean the one," Amanda spun Emma around, "where I lead us into the arena, do some amazing tricks—and you are my sidekick?"

"No," Emma said, batting her eyelashes. "I believe that it's the one where I do some amazing tricks, you're *my* sidekick, and I win a ribbon for my fabulous horseback riding skills!"

This time they both rolled their eyes and giggled.

"What about Bess?" Emma asked, folding her arms.

"I think she and Kiffin are planning some Romeo and Juliet-inspired challenge," Amanda shrugged.

"Yuck!" exclaimed Emma, although she didn't mean to say that out loud.

"Anyway, how could I be in a show without my sidekick?" Amanda said, tilting her head.

"Really!" Emma knew this was Amanda's way of saying sorry. Accepting Amanda's offer was Emma's way of forgiving.

"After tomorrow's 'Fun and Games' challenges," Amanda insisted, "we'll decide on our challenge. I already have a few tricks in mind for my—I mean—*our* big finish!"

?
What big trick would
you do?

Jumping Tips

Good balance is the basis of confident and successful jumping. The correct jumping position is needed so that your horse can keep in balance, too.

Hands
Move your hands up the reins, keeping your arms supple.

Position
Lean your upper body forward, using your back and legs.

Exercises on the lunge
Try out these exercises to improve coordination and increase your suppleness: put your hands on your hips and twist your body from the waist; and hold your hands out and circle them alternately, or both together.

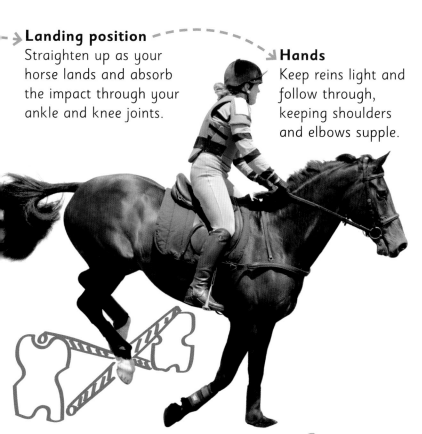

Landing position
Straighten up as your horse lands and absorb the impact through your ankle and knee joints.

Hands
Keep reins light and follow through, keeping shoulders and elbows supple.

Jumping seat
For jumping, bend forward from your hips and keep your head up, shorten stirrups and keep your lower legs in place with your toes up and ankles supple. Practice the balanced jumping position at a standstill.

Mythical Horses

Myths and legends are full of stories about horses with supernatural powers and some with fabulous, magical extra features.

C is for Centaur. This warrior beast had the body of a man and the body and legs of a horse.

H is for Hippocamp. This underwater creature had the head and front legs of a horse and a fish's tail.

H is for Hippogryph. This winged horse with the head and upper body of an eagle was extremely fast and able to fly around the world.

K is for Karkadann. The unicorn of Persia had a rhinoceros' horn and was a fierce beast that could only be tamed by a dove's coo.

P is for Pegasus. This pure white winged stallion grew from the blood of the snake-haired Gorgon Medusa.

T is for Trojan horse. This huge wooden horse was the trap set by the Greek soldiers, tricking the people of Troy and ending the long war.

U is for Unicorn. This magical white horse with a large, spiraling horn on its forehead was a symbol of purity.

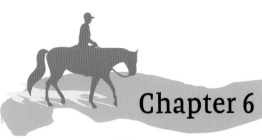

Chapter 6

Fun and Games

The morning's show-and-tell practice flew by much too quickly for Emma and her camp mates. They each took turns leading the class in circles, half circles, diagonals and figure eights, posting into trots, and grumbling about camp coming to an end.

During one of the last trots of the day, Emma felt as if Cinnamon were feeling the same way—and wanting something more from her.

"What is it, Girl?" Emma leaned forward to ask Cinnamon.

Just as Emma finished asking the

question, Cinnamon provided the answer. She picked up the pace and tried nudging them into a canter.

"Whoa!" Emma shortened her reins. She quickly turned Cinnamon and herself into the center of the arena to slow them down.

"Is everything all right?" asked Penny, catching up with Emma.

"Yes, we're fine!" Emma nodded her head and she meant it. "I think Cinnamon tried showing me what we could do together if I came back. We might have cantered or galloped, but I'm not sure."

"I told you that Cinnamon would ask you to push yourself," Penny reminded Emma. "I'm glad you redirected her. Nice work! You two can try cantering when you come back."

Penny's comments seemed to lift Emma's and Cinnamon's spirits. Together, they contently trotted back into the circle.

Annie rode alongside Emma, "If you're not the most improved rider at vacation camp—I'd say you're in the top two!"

Emma blushed, "I can't take all of the credit, can I, Cinnamon?"

Cinnamon snorted.

"*When horse and rider share one heart!*" Emma finally realized what that meant.

The mess hall buzzed with excitement over the afternoon's "Fun and Games" challenges. Some riders were still looking for partners. Emma was relieved she had found hers.

Emma found Amanda sitting with Bess and Kiffin. She had an ice bag on her hand.

"What happened to you?"

"It's nothing," said Amanda, stretching out her fingers.

"It could have been something," Kiffin said, hugging Bess. It was the first time Emma heard him speak to anyone besides Bess.

"Bess and I were racing to take the lead," Amanda sighed, "and when

I tugged a little too hard on Pepper's reins to slow down to get out of Bess's way, he jerked me forward—and I jammed my finger."

"I'm sorry," said Emma, examining Amanda's hand.

"It scared us both, but…" Bess confessed.

"They've recovered really well," remarked Pearl, as she stopped to check on the girls. "Sometimes we forget they're 1,000-pounds animals. When we forget, they remind us!"

After lunch, Pearl declared the games officially open, "Welcome to today's 'Fun and Games,' or 'Gymkhana,' as they've been called for a long time."

"Each pair will compete in five 'Fun and Games' challenges, stressing *fun,* but not at the expense of safety!" Penny warned.

"When you have completed all five challenges," Annie added, "you'll need to fill in your scorecard, hand it in, and receive your certificate."

Emma looked at Amanda as she changed into the matching sweatshirt,

turtleneck, horseshoe earrings, and hair ribbon under the bleachers, and smiled. She felt she had already won a prize.

"This is only for 'Fun and Games,'" Amanda reminded, fixing the ribbon on her braid. "We're not going to make a habit out of dressing the same."

"We have the balloon challenge first," Emma said, checking her scorecard. "That sounds like fun!"

"Yep!" Amanda hooked arms with Emma. "But the *real* fun will happen tomorrow!"

Time for Gymkhana

These mounted games challenge young riders to test a range of their riding skills.

Paddock Promises
"Fun and Games" challenges

Balloons

A timed race in which riders push a row of balloons along the ground with a sharp stick.

Egg-and-spoon

A test of balance and agility as riders walk between two points holding an egg on a spoon.

Flags

A relay race in which flags are passed from one team member to another.

Poles

Riders are timed as they zigzag through poles.

Potatoes

The goal is to drop potatoes into a bucket. A point is given for each potato in the bucket.

Paddock Promises
"Fun and Games" arena

Flags

Balloons

Egg-and-spoon

Center

Potatoes

Poles

Paddock Promises
"Fun and Games" scorecard

	Balloons	Flags	Poles	Potatoes	Egg-and-spoon
Amanda					
Emma					

Teamwork
The points of each team member will be added together for the final score.

After an uneventful "Fun and Games," Emma and Amanda were lucky to secure the last slot to perform in the challenges section of the show.

"It must be our lucky horseshoe earrings," Emma said, flashing her earlobes at Seth. Seth nodded.

"Should we choose one, two, or a combination?" Amanda asked, grabbing a pencil and paper and handing them to Emma.

"Why don't we each choose one?" Emma drew their plan and talked at the same time, "I choose potatoes…"

"I choose poles, and as for my trick…" Amanda pointed, "could we have a container of flags placed here?"

"Sure thing!" Seth took a pen from his cap and jotted down a note.

"Aren't you going to tell *me* what you're planning?" asked Emma. "And what am I supposed to do during your trick?"

"We'll run through it during tomorrow's dress rehearsal. We have the other two nailed down, so now…" Amanda looked at her watch.

"It's time for 'Dinner and Velvet,'" Emma squealed. "We're watching *National Velvet* projected on to the stable wall, eating pizza, and tucking in our horses!"

"I'd love to join you, but," Amanda pulled out her hair ribbon, "I want to spend the last evening with Bess and the other riders in our group. You understand, don't you?"

"We did spend lots of time together today," Emma said, smiling. She nodded her head, "I understand."

"And tomorrow," Amanda promised, "we're going to knock everyone's socks off, so wear two pairs!"

The stable was filled with its usual sweet smells of hay, manure, and air freshener, but it included the aroma of pizza.

"I don't get it." Olive took two plates and handed one to Emma. "Why pizza?"

"It's because the horse in the movie and the book, *National Velvet,* is named The Pie, you see," Emma explained, grabbing silverware and extra napkins, "and the main character, Velvet Brown, falls madly in love with him, and…"

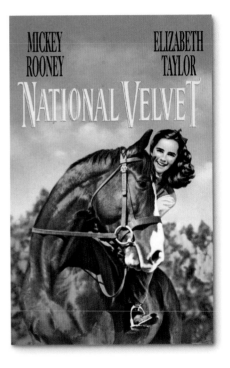

"La, la, la!" Olive covered her ears. "Don't spoil the ending."

"Who wants pizza?" Pearl asked, serving up a large pizza, along with a bowl of fruit to share with the horses.

"And some Sweet Dreams red velvet cupcakes," Emma insisted. "I shared our signature recipe!"

The horses loved the company and treats, especially Cinnamon. She kept poking her head out of her stall, wanting a neck rub and another chunk of apple.

For most of the movie, Emma paid attention to Cinnamon and prepped her for tomorrow.

"We've got a big day ahead with our demonstration, our challenge, and some trick Amanda has planned. So be ready for anything—except saying goodbye!" Emma wiped away tears with her hands.

Cinnamon licked Emma's salty tears with her warm tongue and tried laying her head on her shoulder. Emma thought Cinnamon might be trying to tell her that she was not saying goodbye either.

"But we can say good night," Emma rubbed Cinnamon's neck once more, and kissed her for the millionth time.

National Velvet Review

In 1944, the movie **National Velvet** was released. It was directed by Clarence Brown. Based on the book by Enid Bagnold published in 1935, this is the story of a 12-year-old girl named Velvet Brown and a spirited young horse named The Pie.

Velvet wins her horse in a raffle and is determined to train him to compete in England's Grand National Steeplechase. Velvet is given help from a young former jockey now working for her father.

On the day of the race, Velvet disguises herself as a jockey and rides The Pie to victory, but faints just after the finish.

A doctor discovers her true identity and Velvet and The Pie become headline news and world famous.

Cast

Mickey Rooney
Elizabeth Taylor
Donald Crisp
Jackie Jenkins
Anne Revere
Juanita Quigley
Angela Lansbury

Scenes

Velvet Brown, dressed as a jockey, meets with Mi Taylor at the Grand National Steeplechase before the race.

The Brown family shares a meal with Mi Taylor, the new hired help.

Amazing Horse Facts

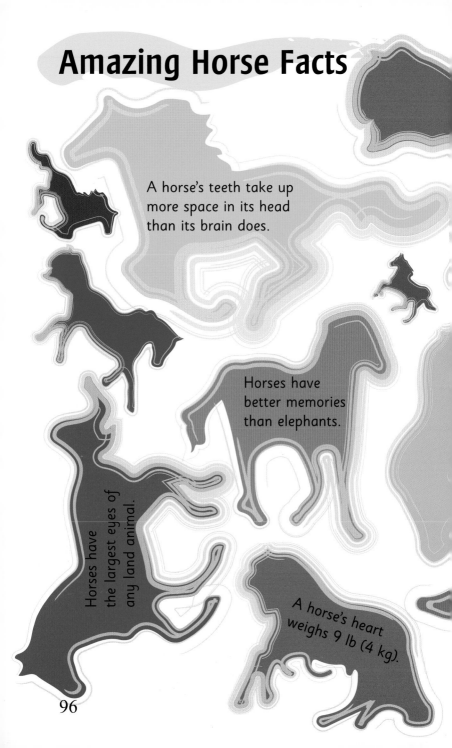

A horse's teeth take up more space in its head than its brain does.

Horses have better memories than elephants.

Horses have the largest eyes of any land animal.

A horse's heart weighs 9 lb (4 kg).

Horses have binocular vision, but they can also see different things in each eye.

There are about 75 million horses in the world.

The name "Philip," and the feminine version, "Philippa," mean "lover of horses."

A horse typically sleeps two and half to three hours a day.

In Australia, there were no horses until 1788.

97

Chapter 7

Show Stopper

"Amandaaaaaaa!" Emma stood over her sister's bed. "You've missed breakfast and dress rehearsal is in 45 minutes. You cannot be late!"

"Don't worry about me," Amanda's voice was muffled under the pillow. "I need a few more minutes of shut-eye. The trail-riding party ran later than expected."

Emma now understood what had kept Amanda out so late.

"I'm going to set the alarm for 15 minutes. Promise me you won't hit the snooze button! We still have to go through our routine again, and…"

"Now I have 14 minutes!" Amanda huffed. "Go! It's our last morning here, and your last with Cinnamon…"

"Well, actually, it's not, if…" Emma started and then stopped.

Amanda pleaded, "Now I only have 13 minutes!"

Emma left and headed for the arena.

"Two-legged and four-legged friends," announced Pearl, standing at the special podium set up for the show, "please take your places for our 'Horse Show-and-Tell' dress rehearsal!"

"We'll start with the beginners, advanced beginners, then the intermediate groups demonstrating their skills," instructed Penny, "and then we'll invite the 'Fun and Games' challenge groups to practice center stage."

Emma kept her eyes peeled to the arena's entrance. She could not believe Amanda had not arrived yet.

"Hey!" exclaimed Olive tapping Emma on the shoulder. "What are you looking for?"

"Amanda! I tried dragging her out of bed." Emma latched her helmet and sighed. "Guess I should stop worrying so much about her and concentrate more on myself. Whoa!"

The words she had spoken surprised Emma as they came out.

"Sounds like camp has done your riding and you some good!" Olive grinned.

"I think you're right!"

Emma sat taller on her saddle. "Thanks to three parts Paddock Promises and one part Cinnamon."

"Now," Pearl continued, "let's have the show of our lives!"

"Please meet our beginning riders," Pearl read from a script. "Each of our riders and their horses have been working hard all week to develop the skills you're seeing now."

Each rider saluted to the empty seats, which would be filled in less than two hours.

"First, the riders will be demonstrating their horse-control skills," narrated Penny.

Emma and Olive took turns leading their camp mates in turning right, turning left, making full and half circles, diagonals, and through a zigzag of cones.

"Don't try this at home, folks. Well, unless you first come to Paddock Promises, that is!" Pearl joked.

Upon rounding the last cone, Emma led the riders back into a circle to begin posting and a slow trot.

"Next, our riders will demonstrate a slow trot." Penny nodded to the riders to begin. "A trot is a quicker gait than a walk, and a bumpy ride at first!"

"Like life…" Pearl paused for effect, "horseback riding's full of ups and downs!"

"Let's go for a trot, Cinnamon," Emma whispered. "Nice and easy!"

Emma rose up and down more confidently than ever before. At long last, Emma and Cinnamon were in complete unison.

"So, that's how we do it!" Emma gulped.

"Let's give a hand to our beginning riders," encouraged Penny, starting the applause. "I think we'll see more of them in the future!"

Amanda missed the dress rehearsal and the first half of the "Horse Show-and-Tell." She did, however, make it just in time for Emma and her challenge.

"I'm here, I'm here!" Amanda said, as she mounted her horse. "Mom, Dad, and Mrs. Bauer are here, too. They are sitting in the front row. We're going to do great and just wait for my trick!"

"Do you think," Emma spotted her parents and waved, "you should skip the trick, since we haven't practiced…?"

"And give up on our horse-sized dream?" Amanda huffed.

"What am I supposed to do while you're doing your trick?" Emma asked, shrugging her shoulders.

"Wait for me in the center of the arena for my… I mean our standing ovation. Trust me!" Amanda prompted.

"I guess. I mean, yes!" Emma did trust her. She wanted to be Amanda most days, but today things felt different.

Emma wondered if Amanda was more interested in *her* horse-sized dream, not *theirs*.

"For our final 'Horse Show-and-Tell Fun and Games' challenge, we have a special sister act from Collingbourne," Pearl built up the anticipation. "Let's give a big hand for Amandaaaaaa and Emmaaaaaa!"

To begin, Amanda led the two of them to their first challenge—the poles. One at a time, Emma and Amanda rounded each pole with the precision of seasoned horse women, surprising even themselves.

"Looking good, Emma," Amanda cheered. "Now it's potato time."

"One potato," Emma counted as she picked up a potato, rode to the bucket, and carefully leaned down to drop it in.

"Two potatoes, three potatoes, four!" Amanda raced past Emma for another potato. Amanda's speed grew with each potato and alarmed Emma.

"Slow down, Amanda," Emma threw her voice like a ventriloquist, "you'll lose control!"

"Don't be silly," Amanda scowled. "Get ready for my trick!"

As the crowd grew louder, thanks to encouragement from Seth and Olive, Emma's heart beat faster, watching and waiting for what Amanda would do.

"Watch this!" Amanda raced to the three flags placed in a barrel. She grabbed one of the flags, raced back to Emma, and handed it to her. Next, she raced back for the others.

Then, suddenly, Amanda stood up in her stirrups, holding a flag in each of her outstretched arms and rode around the arena in perfect balance.

The crowd whistled and cheered wildly. Amanda reached her arms up higher and looked as though she was going to touch the sky.

"Oh, my!" Emma wondered where Amanda had learned such a thing and when she was going to stop.

Unexpectedly, Amanda's right foot slipped out of her stirrups, causing her to lose her balance and fall forward.

Amanda was able to toss the flags off to the side and managed to cling to the side of her horse, but barely.

The crowd gasped. Her parents froze. The show came to a complete standstill—but not Emma.

"I don't think this is part of the trick, Cinnamon, but let's go," spurred on Emma, springing into action.

Emma and Cinnamon raced to Amanda's rescue. Fearlessly, Emma slipped her foot out of her right stirrup and motioned to Amanda.

"Take my hand and put your left foot into my stirrup!"

Following Emma's directions, Amanda transferred to Emma's horse and the two rode together around the arena.

The crowd jumped to their feet and gave them a rousing standing ovation.

"Now that's what I call a real show-stopper!" Pearl whooped. "Remember, you saw it here first!"

Horse Competitions

Dressage
A riding test to demonstrate a horse's training, obedience, and style.

Show jumping
A timed course around an arena of various fences to jump.

Flat racing
A race around a flat track, testing a horse's stamina and speed.

Jump racing

A race around a course with specially built fences to jump. This event is also called steeplechase.

Polo

A ball game where two teams of four players use long-handled mallets to score goals.

Carriage driving

An event where up to four horses pull a light carriage around obstacles.

Working with Horses

People have worked with horses since ancient times. Horses have speed and strength, which has helped to get jobs done.

Show dray horses
Since medieval times, big, powerful dray horses have pulled heavy cartloads. Special harnesses were designed for the horses to lean into the work. Today, these impressive horses demonstrate their muscular strength at horse shows.

Cattle driving

For centuries, horses have been used for rounding up scattered cattle and other animals and moving them as a herd across country on to other land. American cowboys in the 1800s perfected the skills of mounted cattle driving, which modern cowboys continue to use today.

On the farm

Until recently, horses were the main source of power on farms around the world. They were used to plow the land, sow the crops, and bring in the harvest. Horses were also used to rotate shafts for grinding flour in mills.

Help a Horse

Make a difference to thousands of horses worldwide by supporting us in raising awareness, changing policies, and improving practices to make the lives of horses better.

How to help horses

 Find cures for horse diseases.

 Prevent excessive whip use.

 Care for retired sport horses.

 Improve bridle paths.

 Campaign for safer routes.

 Rescue neglected horses.

Horse campaigns

Join other volunteers around the world to help raise awareness, fund-raise, and pass on information about horse welfare.

Find out more >

Bridle paths

Off-road riding should be safe, with a network of plenty of places to ride. We are involved in consultations to protect and improve access to routes and open up public rights of way.

Find out more >

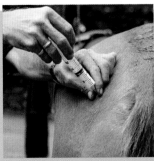

Vaccinations

Disease is one of the greatest threats to horse health. Research, regulating horse movement, and vaccination programs will prevent infectious diseases and their spread across boundaries.

Find out more >

Sport horses

We work in partnership with those who own, train, ride, and take care of sport horses. In retirement, the horse community needs to continue to provide responsible provision.

Find out more >

115

Epilogue

"Amazing! How did you think…?" Amanda dismounted in shock.

"I didn't think; I reacted." Emma dismounted and secured their horses. "You were in trouble and I'd do anything for you!"

Amanda hugged Emma. This time, she didn't want to let go.

"How did I get so lucky to have you as my sister?"

"We're both lucky!" Emma squeezed Amanda, and pointed to a sandy stampede of people heading their way.

The two froze like Sweet Dreams ice-cream cakes preparing to be served.

"Where on earth did you come up with such a show stopper?" asked Pearl, pinning special ribbons to Emma and Amanda.

"I don't think," Penny professed, "I've seen anything like that in all my years of 'Horse Show-and-Tells,' or in any of my competitions!"

"I know a bakery that would like to sponsor you both," Emma and Amanda's parents said at the same time.

"How about a whole club?" Mrs. Bauer pushed her way into the center. "Because when I post this on the school website, just think of all the riding and good we can do!"

"Speaking of good," said Emma's mother, pulling Emma aside, "Annie told me about the special riders and you! I think Sweet Dreams could manage without you for a few days.

"You can?" Emma melted, imagining future possibilities, even owning her own horse. "Do you think…?"

"Let's not put the cart before the horse, but we'll see," giggled Emma's mother.

"Can I go and tell Cinnamon?"

Emma didn't wait for an answer, and dashed off to the stables.

"Where your horse-sized dreams become reality!" exclaimed Emma, as she hugged Cinnamon, remembering the words on the wall again. "They really don't horse around, do they?"

Horse Club Quiz

See if you can remember the answers to these questions about what you have read.

1. What is the name of Emma's family's bakery?

2. What is a dandy brush used for when grooming?

3. What was the Paddock Promises promise?

4. Should a saddle be carried with the pommel toward or away from your elbow?

5. How many beats does a canter have?

6. What is the name of the course in which horses help people with different types of special needs?

7. What was the name of the movie that was watched and in what year was it released?

8. Can you recall the names of the five "Fun and Games" challenges?

9. What is the meaning of the names Philip and Philippa?

10. What is the name of the competition where the horse and rider demonstrate obedience and style?

11. What breed of horse has stamina for long distances and is surefooted for jumping?

12. What did Amanda use for the final trick?

13. What is the only thing that can tame the Karkadann, a fierce Persian unicorn with a rhinoceros horn?

14. What were the names of the two horses that Aimé Tschiffley took on his journey?

15. How much does a horse's heart weigh?

Answers on page 125.

How to Start Your Own Horse Club

If you belong to a group of horse-loving people, why not start your own horse club? Ask an adult to be your supervising leader.

1 Goal of the group

Decide what brings you all together and write a statement.

Examples of goals can be:

- we are interested in finding out more about breeds.
- we want to learn about horse competitions.
- we want to help horses.
- we want to share horse stories.

2 Meeting place and time

Groups often meet once a month to keep things happening throughout the year. Choose a suitable place, such as a school classroom or someone's home. Once or twice a year you could meet in a fun place, such as a restaurant. Always make sure that there are two or more adults with you.

3 Publicity

Let others know about your group so that new members can join. Design flyers with details about when you meet. Provide the contact name and phone number of the supervising adult. Ask your school if you can distribute the flyers.

4 The meetings

Ideas for what to do at meetings could include:
- guest speakers from a local stable yard, trainers, breeders, competitors, vets, and tack store owners.
- make T-shirt designs.
- practice judging a class of horses on a televised competition.
- watch movies that feature horses or talk about famous horse stories.
- find out about national and international horse associations.

5 Outings

A couple of times a year, plan an outing. Places to visit could include visiting a farrier or a saddle maker, going to a horse show, and visiting a stable yard or a tack store.

6 Fund-raising

Plan fund-raising events for horse charities or for funding your own outings. Ideas could include: hosting bake sales, finding sponsors, car washing at local vets, or spending a day helping out at a local stable yard.

7 Set a goal

A goal can build friendships and teamwork as you all share in achieving something together. Examples could be a fund-raising target or a good community service. Have fun!

Glossary

Bit
A piece of metal attached to the bridle that is put into a horse's mouth, allowing for the rider to control the horse's movement.

Bleachers
A tier of planks that form seats in an open-air sports arena.

Braid
Woven strips of ribbon or strands of hair.

Breed
Subdivision of a type of living thing by appearance and character.

Bridle path
An unpaved track suitable for riding or leading horses, but not suitable for cars.

Dismount
To get down from a horse.

Girth
A band or strap around an animal's body used to fasten something on its back, such as a saddle.

Hippotherapy
A form of therapy that involves horseback riding.

Lunge
A long rope attached to a horse and held by someone a distance away. It is used for exercising and training.

Muzzle
The mouth, jaws, and nose of an animal.

Ovation
An enthusiastic applause praising someone's skill.

Pommel
The upper front part of a saddle.

Sanctuary
A place where animals are brought to live and be protected for the rest of their lives.

Shift
A period of time at work.

Sidekick
A close friend who joins another on an adventure or for a challenge.

Stirrups
A pair of metal loops with a flat base hanging on the straps from a horse's saddle for the rider's feet.

Therapy
Treatment such as exercises to help someone with special needs.

Vaccination
The use of medicines injected to prevent specific diseases.

Withers
The ridge between the shoulder bones of a horse.

Answers to the Horse Club Quiz:
1. Sweet Dreams; 2. Removing dried mud and sweat;
3. Where your horse-sized dreams become reality!
4. Toward your elbow; 5. Three beats;
6. Hippotherapy; 7. *National Velvet*, 1944;
8. Egg-and-spoon, flags, poles, balloons, and potatoes;
9. Lover of horses; 10. Dressage;
11. Connemara; 12. Flags; 13. A dove's coo;
14. Mancha and Gato; 15. 9 lb (4 kg).

About the Author

Patricia J. Murphy writes for BIG and little people from her writer's studio in Chicago. She has written over 150 children's books, with more on the way, including board books, early readers, picture books, creative nonfiction titles, chapter books, middle grade novels, as well as a growing list of scripts for children's television.

When she is not writing or riding horses, she spends time with her family, dabbles in acting, helps make Raggedy Ann dolls for children in need, plays golf, runs, and visits Ireland every chance she can get. To find out more about her visit **www.patriciajmurphy.com**.

About the Consultant

Dr. Linda Gambrell, Distinguished Professor of Education at Clemson University, has served as President of the National Reading Conference, the College Reading Association, and the International Reading Association. She is also reading consultant to the *DK Readers*.

Here are some other DK Adventures you might enjoy.

Terrors of the Deep
Marine biologists Dom and Jake take
their deep-sea submersible down into the deepest,
darkest ocean trenches in the world.

Star Wars: Jedi Battles
Join the Jedi on their epic adventures and exciting
battles. Meet brave Jedi Knights who fight for
justice across the galaxy.

Star Wars: Sith Wars
Meet the Sith Lords who are trying to take
over the galaxy. Discover their evil plans
and deadly armies.

Index